Tree Hugging Wild Chimes written by Natasha Georgina Faiers.

Natasha Georgina Faiers

BookLeaf Publishing

Presentation by *BookLeaf Publishing*

Web: www.bookleafpub.com

E-mail: info@bookleafpub.com

ISBN: 9789395969024

First edition 2022

DEDICATION

To the wild, The melody and warmth. To the wood, the weather, To the stream the river, To the sun and rain, Of rainbow panes and of late night stars and my boots...

My boots soggy and growing something like Jazzy zinnias crossed with ox-eyed daisies they're retirement my muddy wellies is one of great memories. Recycled into pollination growing wild seeds.

With thanks to every lark and sail. With thanks to The Wildlife Trusts of whom I was recruited to after much enjoyed leisure pursuits both as an employee and as volunteer.

To The Woodland Trust for encouraging and enabling me to be part of the Tree Stories for woods and trees in both 2015 and 2016.

To The English Heritage for the fine adventures and engagement with historical and to the National Trust for the many places of interest especially Constable Country.

To my incredible tutors for lectures and to all the churches of each visit which brought me comfort, inspiration and solace.

To the wild exploration of waterways and the back waters of the Thames path, the river Roach, The river Crouch, the lochs and wields and the experiences of those creatures from butterflies to dormouse.

To engagement with falcons of which the leather and lace of tasselled wings was an incredibly beautiful experience.

To Swan Rescue for doing such incredible work.

To the arts houses, museums and libraries which have such a special super quantity of adventures. May our humble pages greet you with gratitude and healing.

To memories and to adventure.

To all we have missed from sight hounds to book club chats. So many special thanks too to The RNLI Lifeboats and to the Kent Air Ambulance to which do so much for those adventurous occasionally in peril.

Thank you!

ACKNOWLEDGEMENT

Something in particular we highlight is that as an author

Natasha Georgina Faiers is reasserting her maiden name.

*Please note some works were published within the book 'Essex Belongs To Us' in 2017 formerly Natasha Georgina Barrell her marital name.

*Much of Natasha's work has been previously published under the imprints of Remus House also of which reasserting of authorship is deemed to go forward as now by Natasha Georgina Faiers. Those publications under the banners of Anchor books, Spotlights, Triumph House, Women's Words between 1998 and 2019 are limited editions and any previous published work is of separate project works to this collection of poetry.

This collection is a standing collection published in the full entirety of the author Natasha Georgina Faiers submissions prior noted in print of the aforementioned publications before only as individual verses.

This book brings those works together as pages of its own merits as a wide collection of those she has published previously.

PREFACE

It is a small expression of memories, research of historical and recreational escape to the wildlife, the landscape and the wetlands of three counties. It predominantly is about Essex County yet fleetingly visits to Natasha's place of birth in the County of Kent and through parts of East Anglia along the outskirts of the Thames estuary where her family background has her looking a little at ancestry through her personal verses.

In country Gardens

Hay month bloomed with snapdragons;
Draped in highlights pouting pinks.
Lucky lips for bumblebees;
Floral nectars for them to drink.
Silvered osteospermum's twirled;
Porcelain daisies displayed fluted bells. Apricot
sienna gold, tom thumb nasturtiums; Rouged by
summers rays.
Floating on as windswept petals of roses;
Marbled butterflies, blues with stripy trousers.
Whispered breezes to silent wings, Dancing where
the dunnock sings.
Chirrup swallow's graceful gliders;
Curve swifts around a lone tree sidling. Floret starred
borage transform pinks to blues; Welcoming
sundown's sturgeon moon. Ripe blackberries rotund
in natures making;
Juicy rich for the summers baking.
Youngster starlings once buff now have waistcoats
flecked, speckled,
Dotted as velveteen cloak of purple night musk
settles.
These clearer nodes and meteors shimmer; Lyrically
peeping bursts and glitters.
Born fresh as paddling cygnets at the weir; In its
purest essence of loved relaxation, recreations,
Hay month in the gardens such a lovely time of the
year.

Love On The Rocks

Such loveliness, overlooking river runs;

Rag-stone though weathered hints the sun.

Could a Venus beauty shine when moonlight comes?

As a superseded Neptunism, banded rag and hassock pads such views,

Kentish limes, Island cockleshells and skies so blue.

Once a garden terrace;

A lodge upon a hill.

Surrounded beauty in a wild wood where from ancient sea views seeping,

The growing grapevines, goblets filled.

A duty remains, an old Knight still standing on parade,

For the rocky well-worn outline resembling an age old face.

A home, a simple castle,

A thirteenth century kitchen we're dreaming regal feasts, sumptuous tapestries.

Now sits stonework baked like bread rolls where once chamber maids did creep.

As old age sweeps it, still with a sense of atmosphere,

Sundown came and with it wings of rooks, planets sparkling.

As if to serenade a Kings love from a rocky drum tower,

An olden day peek of sails passing, armour and fine affairs.

The marsh tufts of a moments meander,

A love held dear…

Where even a butterfly could spread its wing and to the stars sing so clear.

When It Smells Like Spring Rain

An azure pearl strung with silver dipped,
A blushing sky, mauve and icy blue rolling on
untamed.
Soft white blossoms glistening dew,
A chatty Jay bird opens wings with a splash of cobalt
hues.
A minstrel woodpecker drumming capped in poppy
red, The gliding sweep of pipistrelles beneath a
starlight night ahead.
Beyond crooked eaves of a slanting barn at the brow
of a twilight hill.
Nature so pure and lovely, sometimes full of song and
sometimes quiet and still. My words could not
capture such beauty, though my pen hand tries.
There is such a connection like seeing again for the
first time.
Maybe like the clarity of seeing with a pheasant's
eyes. For I too have seen the harebells frolic with the
breeze,
Where celandine greets the rivers bend.
A pile of rocks disguising toad and frog under the
creeks arched trees,
I have seen the creeping vines displayed in meadow
grass;
Stood in fields of fresh ploughed corn whilst the
sunlit rainbows dance.
I have meandered wandering often and felt the
raindrops fall.
To be, just be at peace when nature comes to call.

As Free As The Wind My Love...

Opening the day,
The sunlight streamed,
Everything a look,
A glint like freshly polished brass.
The sparrow its joyful cheeks so filled with song.
The scented morning like fresh trimmed grass.
With cheeping, tweeting wag-tail swept,
Its mosaic streaks,
Unstructured songs from beaks.
From a reed swayed pond young frogs leapt.
As free as the wind my love…
Onward beyond caves cockle laid and shingled
seaweed sheets,
Shining where the sail boats pass,
The waters glossed.
Like an old compass remembered in a lighthouse loft.
The skyline slightly cracked the seascape,
A feather in the wind twirling,
Tumbled soft.
Clouds defined reflected in a stream like glass.
The pheasants whirling cluck,
The bark of gulls and descending ducks.
Plumage regally bright and seated in a grassy cup.
As free as the wind my love…
Like an old canvas depicting the blend of quills,
Like the ancient mariner that writes of cogs and reels.
As beautifully nature held us with its love.
For a moment still,

Serene heaven touched the earth.
For a moment then the sea did sigh,
Rose up and laid the landscape poised.
A tiny seal pup gone to bathe, To sail away to sea today.
As free as the wind my love.

A Wonder Of Nature

A wonder of nature I see;
A blended canvas sky and sea.
Illuminated in the skies;
In rolling fields,
I rest my eyes.
From mountain hill I look below;
On a pebbled beach sunsets glow. Fresh barley
ploughed, a hungry crow;
Nocturnal wood greets velvet roe.
A wonder of nature I see;
The fluffing buzz of bumblebees, Painted lady on
gentle breeze.
Transformation of rainbow leaves;
Glitter constellations star lights, As badger paw prints
pad the nights,
A wonder of nature I see.

The Half-Moon Light

The half-moon light within bright eyes;
Hummingbird moth's night butterflies.
An air of nature all around;
Its songs truly beautiful sounds.
As trees bristle, creak and sigh;
Splash laps the lake in float and rise.
Twitter as twilight feathers fly;
In hoots of owls mottled soft browns.
The half-moon light; Calling distance foxes howl
cries,
Badger bear paws silver starlight's. Violet shines
nature's background; Silhouette beauty twinkles
proud.
Cloaks of cloud lifting its disguise;
The half-moon light.

Pipistrelle Music
Horseshoe passage wings, Soprano pitched shadows
dusk;
Stars light celestial.

A Quiet Spot To Dream

Dusty journey lane,
A winding patchwork.
In cinnamon, nutmeg and pistachio.
Where blends the scent of hay.
To our toes a blanket mix,
Of guelder-rose in sprigs the rosehips,
For a shaded seat… A scamper of small creature's
feet,
How the perches were alive.
With peck and tweet,
A pip and squeak…
There arc a climbing speckled wood,
A loft of emerald eyes.
Blue lagoon the singing trickled soft to cloudless
skies.
Of my lady's bedstraw,
Musky mallow clumsily drift.
Amidst cornflowers and silken gossamer threads,
How a dusty mud track led… Of sun-kissed freckled
smiles, A quiet spot to dream a while.
A quiet spot to dream.

Steep Hills Rolling

Steep hills rolling Olympians;
Saxon warriors once champions.
In record breakers century degrees;
Bathes the late summers Rossi breeze.
Skylines altered climate wind turns;
Dressed college roofing solar burns.
Open spotlights to claw crab spurs;
Spider, damsels, fritillary heath.
Steep hills rolling… Watch eyes ancient homestead
stations; Hope for rare natures celebrations.
Five-hundred-year-old rooted trees;
Wood turner's spinney house birds, bees.
Worth the clamber learn conservations;
Steep hills rolling.

Under A pink Moon

Under a pink moon sweet peas sway;
Diamond eyes, the Milky Way.
Ursa Major shining its lights;
The Plough, Big Dipper, shine the nights.
Glittering celestial pave;
Mysterious natures wonders.
Beautiful light to sit and gaze;
Calls Tawny owl as he takes flight. Under a pink
moon sweet peas sway; Lovely moons majestic
phases. Glinting on hummingbird daisies; Warms
imaginations delight.
Of elves and fairies all in flight; Romancing the
beautiful waves,
Under a pink moon sweet peas sway.

Natures Glitter glitziest spanned the gems of night;
Reflections laid a silken sea. The crow moon calling
soars, dreams bright;
Glitziest spanned the gems of night.
The polar star journeyman's lights; Meteor showers,
galaxies. Glitziest spanned the gems of night;
Reflections laid a silken sea.

Wildly Romantic

A wild kingdoms majesty his desires peaking;
True passion its appearance like a mirage.
Hearts leaping throbbing elegance;
Awakening nature's pure romance. Tenderly
observing a charm of display; Snow freckled beauty
leading his way.
A velvet love in warm intimacy;
As eyes glisten reflective and amorously.
Eternal adoration is crowned;
The most regal of the forest stands proud.

The Artists Country

We found ourselves in barley grass;
Where poppies grew as our feet passed.
Church tower in a distant sky;
Beyond foggy grass climbing high.
Meadow roses on bramble grasp;
Frame a picture like its stained glass.
Beautiful memories hearts clasp; Holding hands a
colour wash rise.
We found ourselves.
Like snapshots of a time gone past;
Its paint brushed view treasured to last.
Stippled in a running brooks eye; Spotty cow that
goes sidling by.
Inspirations beauty so vast;
We found ourselves.

A Breeze To Treasure

A breeze gallops with a horse;
Distant sails their spinning course.
Along the lane ivy leaf creeps;
As blue birds sing then kiss with beaks.
Billows the springtime's yellow gorse,
Sparkles the river clear as quartz; Giggling and
spluttering its force. Whispering willow bends the
creek; A breeze.
Rugged skyline so soft yet coarse;
Protect our pleasures mine and yours.
With elusive tread young deer leaps;
Bless Gusted Halls cherry tree breeze. Touching
countryside with our hearts;
A breeze.

Ears For Beauty

Beauty sounds like church bells ringing;
Charms of goldfinches chattering.
A xylophone in conker tree;
As dappled wood notes comfort me.
The murmur in starlings soaring; Orchestra to
blossoms falling. Robin serenades pitched mornings;
Butterfly wings flutter fly free.
Beauty sounds… Cheeky woodpecker now laughing;
Then continues hare foot drumming. Drifts rains
pattern splashing like seas; Nightingales choir
musically. The wonder in natures singing;
Beauty sounds.

Blossoms Innocence

Wild cherry and thorn in blossom;
Gold plum rekindled innocence. Skips lambs, gorse
has bloomed in sunbeams; How a tiny fox cubs eyes
gleam. The oak trees refreshed and handsome;
Bluebells gown the woodland madams.
Dancing in and out suns prisms, Leaf unfurl again
lime and green, Wild cherry and thorn.
For the rain song has a fresh hum; Blue skies lift us
feeling gladsome. Celandine brightens flowing
streams; Canopy wings buzz bumble breeze.
Holly blue springs in optimum;
Wild cherry and thorn.

In Hockley Woods

In Hockley woods we take a walk;
Shining birch nests sparrow's wedlock.
Stealth's jay bird his spring acorn seeds;
Autumn treasures sweet chestnut trees.
May flowers as dress foxgloves frocks;
Scented fragrance of peas sweet stalks.
Amusing green woodpecker knocks,
Squirrels bustle in tumbled leaves, In Hockley
woods.
Painted lady flutters her spots;
Blue sky through hornbeam greets cornstalks.
Smart dunnock suited dressed in tweed; Bright jewel
clusters of berried beads.
Listening as ancient coppice talks;
In Hockley woods.

Joyful Days

Joyful days greeting friendly swans;
Proud sail mate Captain waddling on.
Then beautiful little egret;
Wading in the shallows a treat.
The high sun melts like marzipan;
Like the sky was coloured crayon.
Passing yachts and sails of chiffon;
Humid day come night's sweet secrets.
Joyful days,
To the night owl's new liaisons,
Stars twinkle when suns sleepy gone.
Blend skylines like bright nuggets;
Memory gem in my pocket.
Precious to build new dreams upon; Joyful days.

Light On Water

Light on water mouth of the Crouch; Sun raising like
a seal pups snout.
Wagtail lead us along the quay;
Gulls and terns swoop effortlessly. Where boats sat
heeled at the seas pout; Silk sailing ships bobbing
wave's clouts.
Ducks paddled as wash drifted clouts Tea shop
windows sat pastry glazed, Light on water. The
smell of pewter seas rollout; Aboard a tug
sail-makers shout.
Souvenir bottled ships of days;
Rolling skies in platinum phase. Sunshine
shimmering cloudy bouts;
Light on water.

Come Kiss

Beyond The Cockle Sheds
Come kiss beyond the cockle sheds; With sailor's
quoits let lovers wed.
Let's cast off our troubles to sea; Enjoy the light upon
the Leigh.
Together walk and journeys tread;
Watch fishermen's nets casting threads.
Seagulls swooping, their daily bread;
Salty water lapping carefree.
Come kiss.
Delight in sunset as it spreads;
Painting the canvas old town red. Trail the brambles
and the sweet pea; Blackberry fingers and green tea.
Drifting satin boats from the quay;
Come kiss.

The Thatch Found Love

The thatch found love as timber speaks;
Weaving coloured homes winding streets. Charm
quaint doorways and iron lanterns; Rural whimsy in
small taverns. Through the tree cots the church spire
peeks;
The white sails of the windmill creaks.
Like a prize in finest antiques; Gaze the buildings
pretty patterns.
The thatch found love.
Was it once that Turpin did sneak?
Through nocturne nights did silent creep?
Like two spoons its romance does yearn;
As a postcard in an album. Idyllic with its sweet
mystique;
The thatch found love.

Heritage Of His Love

These old walls like sponge, Collecting time and
space.
How different was the world,
When old crowns were set in place?
These steps have felt the feet of many,
This window where love sat,
For history here so compelling,
In the courtyard the blooms remember that.

Of His Love...
My eyes they know his eyes,
For my lips they know his kiss. My cheeks they
know his hands, My heart thumps just for his. With
every blush I am fonder still, With every touch I am
taken.
Whilst he and I have yet to meet.
My dream of him and I remains the hearts seeking.
Yet still my minds quiet time in fond tribute of our
love's tremendous jubilation.

Such Sweet Memories

Such Sweet Memories…
A hint of summer longing sung in sweet tones,
Gentle earthy scents crept the tips of our nose.
As gorse and broom brushed fields mellow,
Well-dressed trunks now spread the wintered gaps in
tumbling hedgerows.
Oh such sweet memories…
The chamomile hills rolled away, Swooping swifts to
the seas.
Sewn in the wild hedge rose,
Neatly brewing shades of leaves.
Where tapestry reaches every well earthed place,
Upon a ridge, to for a while just sit and gaze.
Oh such sweet memories…
Perfumed orchids tempted fox trots,
Serene courting, painted ladies hopped in bug love,
Humming along with the bumbling bees,
Barley grass weaving the breeze.
Oh such sweet memories…
Greened wheat laden autumn promises kissed the
land,
Riding gallant as hare and hand.
Foot falls rhythm echoes naturally,
Rambling along a warm yellow vista beautifully.
The call of the wilds rugged simplicity,
So deeply embraced with nature's melody.
Oh such sweet memories…
Such sweet memories.

With fondness and adoration,

Natasha Georgina Faiers